The 9/11 Terrorist Attacks

AMERICAN LEADERS
THEN AND NOW

Abdo & Daughters
MIDDLE GRADE NONFICTION

An imprint of Abdo Publishing
abdobooks.com

Jessica Rusick

ABDOBOOKS.COM

Published by Abdo Publishing, a division of ABDO, PO Box 398166, Minneapolis, Minnesota 55439. Copyright © 2021 by Abdo Consulting Group, Inc. International copyrights reserved in all countries. No part of this book may be reproduced in any form without written permission from the publisher. Abdo & Daughters™ is a trademark and logo of Abdo Publishing.

Printed in the United States of America, North Mankato, Minnesota.

102020

012021

THIS BOOK CONTAINS
RECYCLED MATERIALS

Design: Kelly Doudna, Mighty Media, Inc.

Production: Mighty Media, Inc.

Editor: Liz Salzmann

Cover Photographs: Doug Mills/AP Images (left), Chad J. McNeeley/Flickr

Interior Photographs: Chad J. McNeeley/Flickr, p. 1; CIV Scott H. Spitzer, USAF/Flickr, p. 37; Doug Mills/AP Images, pp. 1 (left), 7, 12, 13; Evan Vucci/AP Images, pp. 30, 31; Getty Images, p. 23; Helene C. Stikkel/Wikimedia Commons, p. 28; Jim Collins/AP Images, pp. 4, 5, 44; John-Marshall Mantel/AP Images, pp. 16, 17; Mike Derer/AP Images, p. 32; Mike Segar/AP Images, p. 15; MSgt Cecilio Ricardo/Wikimedia Commons, p. 36; Pete Souza/Flickr, p. 38; Robert Spencer/AP Images, p. 14; Shutterstock Images, pp. 19, 34, 35, 43, 45; Teru Iwasaki/ AP Images, p. 33; The White House/Flickr, pp. 1, 41; US National Archives/Flickr, pp. 9, 11, 18, 21, 24, 25, 27; US State Department/Flickr, p. 42

Design Elements: Shutterstock Images

LIBRARY OF CONGRESS CONTROL NUMBER: 2020940244

PUBLISHER'S CATALOGING-IN-PUBLICATION DATA

Names: Rusick, Jessica, author.

Title: American leaders: then and now / by Jessica Rusick

Other title: then and now

Description: Minneapolis, Minnesota : Abdo Publishing, 2021 | Series: The 9/11 terrorist attacks | Includes online resources and index

Identifiers: ISBN 9781532194481 (lib. bdg.) | ISBN 9781098213848 (ebook)

Subjects: LCSH: September 11 Terrorist Attacks, 2001--Juvenile literature. | Acts of terrorism-- Juvenile literature. | United States--Politics and government--Juvenile literature. | United States--History--Juvenile literature.

Classification: DDC 973.9310922--dc23

TABLE OF CONTENTS

As black smoke billows from the Twin Towers of the WTC after terrorists flew airplanes into them, the South Tower (*left*) begins to collapse.

Chapter 1

THE UNITED STATES UNDER ATTACK

On September 11, 2001, the United States suffered the worst terrorist attack in its history. That day, terrorists boarded four commercial airplanes. They hijacked the planes midflight and flew them toward US landmarks. The terrorists flew the first two planes into the 110-story Twin Towers of the World Trade Center (WTC) complex in New York City. Both buildings collapsed less than two hours later. The WTC complex became a 16-acre (6.5 ha) pile of dust and rubble.

The terrorists crashed the third plane into the Pentagon in Washington, DC. The Pentagon is the headquarters of the US Department of Defense. A section of the building later collapsed. The terrorists in the fourth plane were likely also headed for Washington, DC, to target the White House or the US Capitol Building. However, the plane crashed in a Pennsylvania field after passengers and crew stormed the cockpit. Together, these hijackings are known as the 9/11 terrorist attacks.

A Shocked Nation

Nearly 3,000 people were killed in the 9/11 terrorist attacks. The death toll included office workers, first responders, bystanders, and everyone aboard the airplanes. Years later, those who developed diseases from breathing toxic air at the crash sites would be added to this number.

A shocked, frightened nation looked to American leaders after the attacks. National and local leaders comforted and reassured Americans in the immediate aftermath. The president, his advisors, and Congress worked to pass laws that would help victims and keep the United States safe from future threats. And, US intelligence agencies worked to find those responsible for the attacks.

President Bush Learns of the Attacks

On the morning of September 11, President George W. Bush was at Emma E. Booker Elementary School in Sarasota, Florida. He was there to sit in on a reading lesson with students and give a speech about education.

When Bush took office in January 2001, he had become the president of a divided nation. The 2000 election was one of the closest in US history. Bush was only the fourth president to win the presidency while losing the popular vote. So, many people were

When White House chief of staff Andrew Card (*left*) told Bush about the attacks, Bush stayed with the children for a few minutes. He wanted to convey calm, not panic.

unhappy with Bush's election. Bush hoped to earn their respect as president.

Just before Bush entered the Florida classroom, an aide told him that a small plane had crashed into the North Tower of the WTC. At the time, there was not much information available about the crash. Like most people, Bush assumed it was a tragic accident. But as

Bush sat in on the reading lesson, his chief of staff, Andrew Card, went over and whispered in his ear. "A second plane hit the second tower," Card said. "America is under attack."

Vice President Cheney

After leaving the school, Bush rushed to Air Force One, the presidential airplane. The plane took off and headed to an air force base where the president would be protected. During the flight, Bush watched news coverage of the attacks. He also made calls to his advisors.

One call was to Vice President Dick Cheney. Cheney was no stranger to crises. He had held many government positions since 1969. This included serving as secretary of defense under Bush's father, President George H.W. Bush.

Cheney was in the White House during the attacks. For his safety, Secret Service agents quickly had Cheney go to a bunker beneath the White House called the Presidential Emergency Operations Center (PEOC). Over the next hours, Cheney received updates about the attacks from investigators and other officials. Cheney passed the information to Bush. Bush then issued several orders, which Cheney helped carry out.

Airplanes Grounded

To prevent more hijackings, Bush ordered air traffic control agents to stop all civilian air traffic. Starting immediately, no civilian planes could take off from US airports. However, some planes were already in flight. So, Bush told Cheney to have air traffic control contact these planes and instruct them to land at the airports they were closest to.

Any plane that didn't respond would be assumed to be under the control of hijackers. Bush said if that happened, the military should shoot the plane to stop it from reaching its target. It turned out that no planes were shot down.

Other Presidential Advisors

National security advisor Condoleezza Rice was also in the PEOC. Rice was a gifted scholar. She was also the first female and first

Rice (*left*) and Cheney review information about the attacks in the PEOC.

African American national security advisor. In this role, Rice helped Bush plan his foreign policy. From Rice, Bush learned about the attack on the Pentagon.

Bush also called Secretary of Defense Donald Rumsfeld. Rumsfeld led the US Department of Defense at the Pentagon. He was responsible for the nation's military and national security. At first, the president couldn't reach the secretary. Rumsfeld had been in the Pentagon when it was attacked. Rumsfeld was uninjured. But he quickly ran to the crash site and helped survivors escape.

Bush Addresses the American People

Several hours after leaving Florida, Air Force One landed at Offutt Air Force Base in Kansas. There, Bush held a video meeting with several of his advisors. Although his advisors and security team warned against it, Bush insisted on returning to Washington, DC. He wanted the nation to see him leading from the White House.

That evening, Bush made an address to the American people. "Terrorist attacks can shake the foundations of our biggest buildings," Bush said. "But they cannot touch the foundation of America." Bush and his advisors had two major tasks ahead of them. First, they had to help the victims of the attacks and protect Americans from future threats. And, they had to find those responsible for the attacks.

Bush gave his national address from the Oval Office in the White House.

On September 14, Giuliani (*left*) visited the WTC site with Bush (*center*), Pataki (*second from left*), Senator Charles Schumer (*second from right*), and New York City Fire Commissioner Thomas Van Essen.

Chapter 2

NEW YORK LEADERS

When the South Tower collapsed, New York City mayor Rudolph "Rudy" Giuliani was in an office building two blocks away, trying to call Cheney to discuss the attacks. Along with thousands of other people, Giuliani left that area of the city on foot. He walked calmly down streets filled with dust.

Giuliani went to a building two miles away, where he set up a command center to respond to the disaster. Giuliani and his staff made sure subways were routed away from the WTC. And, they ensured that food, bulldozers, and lights were delivered to the site.

Many Americans were moved by Giuliani's calm, competent leadership. He soon became known as "America's Mayor." In the next weeks, Giuliani attended dozens of victims' funerals. He apologized for not being able to attend more.

Governor Pataki

New York governor George E. Pataki was also in New York City during the attacks. As the state's governor, his main office was in the capital, Albany. But at the time, he was visiting New York City. Soon after the attacks, Pataki ordered that doctors, nurses, and medical supplies be sent to the WTC. He also closed New York City schools and postponed voting in the primary election scheduled for that day.

Pataki's security team wanted to evacuate the governor to Albany. However, Pataki refused. He felt it was important to stay in New York City. In the aftermath, Pataki visited a hospital near the WTC. There, he comforted those who had survived the attacks.

Cleanup and Rebuilding

After the attacks, the WTC site became known as Ground Zero. Cleanup at Ground Zero began immediately. Fire Chief Frank P. Cruthers helped supervise the cleanup. Cruthers and other fire department officials assigned workers to different areas to sort through and remove debris. Fire department officials also brought in engineers and construction workers to tear down the remains of the damaged buildings. Cruthers' leadership helped keep the cleanup moving smoothly.

In 2002, Cruthers (*left*) became Chief of Department for the second time. He had also held that role in 1996.

In November 2001, Governor Pataki and Mayor Giuliani created the Lower Manhattan Development Corporation (LMDC). This group's job was to come up with a plan to rebuild the WTC complex and surrounding area. On January 1, 2002, Giuliani's term as mayor ended. Michael Bloomberg became mayor.

On his first day in office, Bloomberg spent time with the workers at Ground Zero. He then started working with the LMDC to rebuild Ground Zero. By 2004, the group had selected designs for several new buildings at the WTC. The LMDC also chose a design for a 9/11 memorial.

However, the LMDC's projects were delayed by arguments and redesigns. By 2006, it seemed that construction on the 9/11 memorial would never begin. That year, Bloomberg became chairman of the 9/11 Memorial & Museum. Over the next years, he worked to lower the project's budget. And, he raised $450 million to help fund the memorial. Thanks to Bloomberg's leadership, the 9/11 Memorial opened to the public on September 12, 2011. In May 2014, the 9/11 Memorial Museum opened.

Bloomberg (*third from right*) greets visitors on the opening day of the 9/11 Memorial.

Firefighter John Burnside's widow (*left*) and office worker William Minardi's daughter and widow attended a press conference about the VCF.

Chapter 3

HOMELAND SECURITY

The federal government quickly took steps to respond to the attacks. Although Democrats and Republicans had fought bitterly about the 2000 election, members of Congress were ready to put aside their differences to help the American people. On September 21, 2001, Congress passed the Air Transportation Safety and System Stabilization Act. This act included the September 11th Victim Compensation Fund (VCF). The fund gave money to people who were injured in the 9/11 terrorist attacks and to the families of those who were killed. In return for the money, fund recipients agreed to not sue the airlines that owned the hijacked planes.

Protecting the Country

The government also took measures to prevent future terrorist attacks. On September 22, 2001, Bush appointed Pennsylvania governor Tom Ridge Director of the Office of Homeland Security. The office oversaw and coordinated a national strategy to protect the country from

PIVOTAL PERSON: TOM RIDGE

Tom Ridge was a Vietnam War veteran who had served for six terms in the House of Representatives before becoming governor of Pennsylvania in 1995. As governor, Ridge was known for his efforts to improve his state's economy and education system. As Director and then Secretary of Homeland Security, Ridge helped improve the country's emergency responsiveness, border security, intelligence analysis, and more.

terrorism and respond to any future attacks. In November 2002, the Office of Homeland Security became part of the president's cabinet as the Department of Homeland Security (DHS), and Ridge became the first Secretary of Homeland Security. The DHS combined several existing agencies and services into one large agency. These included the US Coast Guard and the Federal Emergency Management Agency.

Ridge (*left*) meets with Bush at the White House. Ridge served as Secretary of Homeland Security until February 1, 2005.

In the month after 9/11, Congress also passed the USA PATRIOT Act. Bush signed the act into law on October 26, 2001. The USA PATRIOT Act expanded the power of US intelligence and law enforcement agencies to combat terrorism. This allowed the agencies to monitor terror-related telephone and internet communication. It also allowed the agencies to obtain records from businesses, including schools and hospitals, if the records pertained to a terror investigation.

TSA agents screen passengers and baggage at 450 airports in the United States.

Increasing Airport Security

In November 2001, Congress passed the Aviation and Transportation Security Act. The law required that airplane cockpit doors be made stronger and kept locked during flight. This was to make it harder for hijackers to gain control of an airplane. The law also established the Transportation Security Administration (TSA), which became part of the DHS.

The TSA standardized security procedures in airports across the country. Before the TSA existed, airports and airlines were responsible for their own security. So, procedures varied from airport to airport and airline to airline. In addition to standardizing procedures, TSA security officers implemented new measures to make plane travel safer.

For example, all carry-on and checked bags had to be screened for potential weapons. Prior to the 9/11 terrorist attacks, checked luggage was rarely screened. Also, since it was reported that the hijackers used box cutters as weapons during the hijackings, the TSA prohibited bringing small knives or other sharp tools onto planes in carry-on bags.

2001 VS. TODAY

To prepare for the 9/11 terrorist attacks, some of the hijackers attended US flight schools to learn how to fly commercial airplanes. At the time, there was little security at such schools. Today, the TSA thoroughly checks the background, criminal history, and immigration status of US flight school students.

Over time, the TSA added new rules as new threats emerged. In December 2001, a man hid a bomb in one of his shoes to smuggle it onto an airplane. After the plane took off, he tried to light the bomb with a cigarette lighter. Luckily, he was stopped before he could succeed. Soon after that incident, the TSA started requiring passengers to remove their shoes at security checkpoints so the shoes could be scanned for explosives.

FBI Investigation

As Congress worked to pass legislation in response to the 9/11 terrorist attacks, US intelligence agencies launched investigations into the attacks. One agency was the Federal Bureau of Investigation (FBI). It was headed by Robert Mueller. Mueller had worked in criminal justice for decades. He had experience investigating everything from small crimes to terrorist bombings. Mueller had been appointed FBI Director just one week before the 9/11 terrorist attacks. To discover who was responsible for the attacks, Mueller launched the largest investigation in the FBI's history. The investigation was codenamed PENTTBOM, which stood for "Pentagon/Twin Towers Bombing."

Mueller (*left*) worked with (*second from left to right*) Central Intelligence Agency (CIA) Director George Tenet, Attorney General John Ashcroft, and Ridge to strengthen national security after the 9/11 terrorist attacks.

9/11 BY THE NUMBERS

FBI agents investigated 500,000 leads during PENTTBOM. They also conducted more than 167,000 interviews, collected 150,000 pieces of evidence, and took more than 170,000 photos.

PENTTBOM was wide-ranging. About 7,000 FBI agents and other staff members were involved. They worked to recover victims and evidence from the WTC, the Pentagon, and the Pennsylvania crash site. Agents also worked to gather information about those responsible for the attacks.

On September 27, 2001, the FBI released photographs of the 19 hijackers who carried out the attacks. The FBI asked the public to come forward with any information about the hijackers. Mueller also sent agents to 30 countries to pursue leads on the terrorists.

Al-Qaeda

Within days of the attacks, US intelligence officials confirmed the hijackers were members of al-Qaeda. Al-Qaeda is an Islamist terrorist group that formed in Afghanistan. Its followers believe in enforcing strict laws based on an extreme interpretation of Islam. Al-Qaeda members often use violence to achieve this goal. People who follow Islam are called Muslims. Most Muslims do not agree with al-Qaeda's views. In fact, many Muslims think al-Qaeda's beliefs and actions go against the teachings of Islam.

Waleed M. Alsheri

Mohammed Atta

Wail M. Alshehri

Abdulaziz Alomari

Satam M.A. al-Suqami

Ahmed Alnami

Ahmed Ibrahim A. al Haznawi

Ziad Samir al-Jarrah

Saeed Alghamdi

Khalid Almihdar

Majed Moqed

Nawaf Alhazmi

Salem Alhazmi

Hani Hanjour

Marwan Alshehhi

Ahmed Alghamdi

Mohand Alshehri

Hamza Alghamdi

Fayez Rashid
Ahmed Hassan
al-Qadi Banihammad

FBI photos of the suspected hijackers. They are arranged in rows by which flight they were on. *From top to bottom*: Flight 11, Flight 93, Flight 77, and Flight 175.

The war cabinet met at Camp David on September 15, 2001. Members included (*left to right*) Bush, Secretary of State Colin Powell, and Rumsfeld.

Chapter 4

LEADING THE WAR ON TERROR

Immediately after the 9/11 terrorist attacks, Bush formed a war cabinet to review information about the attacks and plan a response. There were 13 members of the war cabinet, including Cheney, Rice, Rumsfeld, and Central Intelligence Agency (CIA) director George Tenet.

The war cabinet focused on Afghanistan, since that was where al-Qaeda was based. At the time, most of Afghanistan was ruled by an oppressive government called the Taliban. The Taliban protected al-Qaeda and its leader, Osama bin Laden. So, the war cabinet members knew the United States would have to fight the Taliban as well as al-Qaeda.

Four Phases of War

The war cabinet chose US Army General Tommy Franks to plan the war in Afghanistan. Franks had served in the army since 1967, when he fought in the Vietnam War. After the war, Franks rose through the ranks. In June 2000, he became a four-star general and was named commander of the United States Central Command. This command oversees military operations in 25 countries.

Around September 19, Franks presented a four-phase plan. First, US troops would establish bases in countries bordering Afghanistan, including Uzbekistan and Pakistan. Phase two called for air strikes against Taliban and al-Qaeda targets in Afghanistan, such as terrorist training camps. US planes would also drop packets of food in various locations to help Afghan civilians affected by the war.

In phase three, US ground troops would enter Afghanistan. These troops would work with Afghan security forces to take back cities from Taliban control. Another goal was to capture al-Qaeda terrorists, including Osama bin Laden. Following the fall of the Taliban, US troops would help bring stability to the country to prevent future terrorist activity. This would be phase four.

The War on Terror Begins

Bush and the war cabinet approved Frank's plans. On September 20, 2001, Bush spoke before Congress and the nation to announce the war on terror. The war in Afghanistan was part of this effort. However, Bush also vowed to target terrorist groups around the world. Bush called on foreign nations to join the United States in the fight against terrorism.

The war in Afghanistan started with Operation Enduring

Freedom. Air strikes began on October 7. Ground troops entered the country in late October. In the next months, US and Afghan forces worked together to drive the Taliban out of large cities in Afghanistan. Several al-Qaeda and Taliban terrorists were captured or killed. However, Osama bin Laden escaped.

On December 7, US and Afghan forces gained control of Kandahar, the last major Taliban stronghold. Soon, rebuilding efforts began. However, phase four proved difficult. More US troops were deployed to Afghanistan to train Afghan security forces. While troops fought in Afghanistan, a new enemy in the war on terror was identified.

Members of Congress applaud during Bush's address on September 20.

War in Iraq

Bush believed Iraq was another country that could be a source of terrorism. In 2001, Iraq was ruled by a ruthless dictator named Saddam Hussein. Hussein had publicly praised the 9/11 terrorist attacks. And, Hussein's government had long been involved in various terrorist acts around the world. So, Bush and other leaders had wondered if Iraq was involved in the 9/11 terrorist attacks.

Initial intelligence reports found no evidence linking Iraq to the 9/11 terrorist attacks. However, Bush and his advisors believed that Iraq possessed weapons of mass destruction (WMDs). Bush worried that Hussein would give or sell these weapons to terrorists. Bush wanted to invade Iraq to find these WMDs and remove Hussein from power to prevent future threats from Hussein's regime. So, Franks began preparing plans for an invasion of Iraq.

Rumsfeld (*left*) and Franks speak to the press about the status of the war in Iraq.

On October 11, 2002, Congress authorized the Bush administration to declare war on Iraq. Most Republicans voted for this measure. However, the decision divided Democrats. Some worried that the administration was rushing into war.

The Invasion of Iraq

On March 20, 2003, US troops, along with support from the United Kingdom and other allies, invaded Iraq. They quickly defeated Hussein's forces. By April 9, US and Iraqi soldiers had taken control of Iraq's capital city, Baghdad. Hussein went into hiding but was captured later that year. He was tried in an Iraqi court and found guilty of crimes against humanity. Hussein was sentenced to death and executed in 2006.

Meanwhile, on May 1, 2003, Bush declared the military phase of the Iraq War over. As in Afghanistan, efforts now turned to rebuilding the country's infrastructure, government, and military. However, different groups within Iraq were fighting for power. This civil war led to suicide bombings and attacks on religious landmarks.

Some Americans believed Franks had not properly planned for the aftermath of the Iraq invasion. The new Iraqi government and military were not yet strong enough to control the violence and unite the country. Thousands of US and Iraqi troops and hundreds of thousands of Iraqi civilians died in the fighting over the next years.

Thomas H. Kean

The 9/11 Commission swears in witnesses at
its final hearing, held on June 16 and 17, 2004.

Chapter 5

THE 9/11 COMMISSION

While the war in Afghanistan targeted those responsible for the 9/11 terrorist attacks, the full details of how and why the attacks happened were still unclear. Many people thought US intelligence agencies should have known that such a complicated, deadly attack was being planned. Then, it possibly could have been stopped.

To discover more about how the attacks happened, in November 2002 Bush created the National Commission on Terrorist Attacks Upon the United States. Also called the 9/11 Commission, this group's purpose was to undertake an in-depth study of the attacks. Based on its findings, the Commission would make recommendations on how to better prevent terrorist attacks.

Working Together

The 9/11 Commission had ten members and an 81-person staff. The ten Commission members were members of Congress, split evenly between Republicans and Democrats. The group was led by Republican Thomas H. Kean, the former governor of New Jersey, and Indiana congressman Democrat Lee H. Hamilton. Both leaders were committed to making sure the Commission was nonpartisan. Early on, they decided that any recommendations would have to be agreed upon by all ten Commission members.

The Commission examined several topics. One was al-Qaeda's development. Another was how US intelligence agencies had tracked terrorists prior to 9/11. And, the Commission studied how 9/11 emergency responses had been coordinated on September 11.

From March 2003 to June 2004, the Commission held 12 public hearings. In these hearings, survivors and other witnesses testified about their experiences during and after the attacks. The Commission heard from first responders, counterterrorism experts, and many of Bush's advisors, including Rice. The Commission interviewed Bush and Cheney privately.

Kean (*left*) was the chairman of the 9/11 Commission. Hamilton (*right*) was the vice chairman.

The 9/11 Commission Report

In July 2004, the commission delivered its findings in the *Final Report of the National Commission on Terrorist Attacks Upon the United States*, also called the *9/11 Commission Report*. Its main conclusion was that intelligence agencies had underestimated

Negroponte served as Director of National Intelligence from April 21, 2005 to February 13, 2007.

al-Qaeda's threat to the United States. The report made several recommendations for how US intelligence agencies could better protect the nation from future attacks.

One recommendation was to create a Director of National Intelligence position within the government. This position would oversee all 15 federal intelligence agencies. That way, agencies could share information more easily. In December 2004, Congress followed this recommendation when it passed the Intelligence Reform and Terrorism Prevention Act. This bill created a Director of National Intelligence. The act also created the National Counterterrorism Center, an office that works to prevent domestic and international terrorism.

On April 21, 2005, John Negroponte became the first Director of National Intelligence. He had a lot of experience in foreign relations and national security. Prior to this appointment, Negroponte was serving as the US Ambassador to Iraq. He had also been ambassador to several other countries as well as the United Nations. And, Negroponte had served as deputy national security advisor under President Ronald Reagan.

In 2008, demonstrators in St. Paul, Minnesota, protested the war in Iraq. Similar protests occurred in other US cities as well.

Chapter 6

CHANGES IN LEADERSHIP

In late 2008, Bush's second term as president was almost over. He had led the United States through one of the worst disasters in its history. In the days after the 9/11 terrorist attacks, many Americans had been comforted and inspired by Bush's leadership. By late September 2001, Bush's approval rating had been 90 percent. This was the highest approval rating of any president in US history.

An Uncertain Legacy

Bush had to make many tough decisions after 9/11. Some decisions grew less popular over time. For example, the wars in Afghanistan and Iraq had been popular with the public at first. Both wars had early successes. But as the wars dragged on, many Americans disapproved of the continued conflicts.

Another problem for Bush was that US troops never found any WMDs in Iraq. The Bush administration later admitted their information had been wrong. Critics said Bush and his advisors had only shared intelligence that supported going to war.

The USA PATRIOT Act also grew less popular over time. The bill had bipartisan support when it passed. However, in the next years, many lawmakers became concerned that the law gave the government too much power to spy on Americans. By the end of 2008, Bush's approval rating had fallen to 25 percent.

Bush had done his best to lead the nation during a difficult time. His decisions had produced some good and some bad results. Bush's legacy would influence the work of future presidents.

A New President

On January 20, 2009, Barack Obama became the new president of the United States. By this point, support for the wars in Afghanistan and Iraq had declined among the American public. So, one of Obama's campaign promises had been to end the wars.

In 2009, Obama began withdrawing US troops from Iraq. And that December, he said he would begin pulling US troops out of Afghanistan by 2011. In the meantime, however, Afghan forces needed help. They were fighting a new terrorist

Obama taking the oath of office at his inauguration

More than 6,500 US soldiers have died in the wars in Afghanistan and Iraq.

group known as the Islamic State of Iraq. So over the first months of 2010, Obama sent 30,000 more troops to Afghanistan. In December 2011, Obama brought the last US combat troops home from Iraq. However, there were still nearly 100,000 US troops in Afghanistan.

Finding Osama bin Laden

One major success of the Obama administration was finding Osama bin Laden. Bin Laden had been in hiding since 2002. In August 2010, US intelligence operatives finally tracked down his hideout. Bin Laden and his family were living in a large compound in Pakistan. It took several months to form a plan and prepare to capture him.

On May 1, 2011, Obama authorized a team of Navy SEALs to raid the compound to capture bin Laden. Obama and other US security leaders watched live video of the raid from the White House. Bin Laden refused to surrender and ended up being killed. That night, Obama announced bin Laden's death to the nation. Many Americans felt that bin Laden had finally been brought to justice for his role in the 9/11 terrorist attacks.

First Lady Michelle and Barack Obama visit the Flight 93 National Memorial. The boulder marks the location of the main impact of the plane.

Supporting and Honoring 9/11 Victims

On January 2, 2011, Obama signed the James Zadroga 9/11 Health and Compensation Act of 2010. This act reactivated the VCF, which had ended in 2004. The VCF was reactivated to help people who were still suffering from the effects of the 9/11 terrorist attacks. For example, many survivors and first responders who worked at the crash sites developed illnesses after 9/11. They suffered respiratory diseases and cancer caused by toxic air at Ground Zero, the Pentagon, and the Pennsylvania crash

9/11 BY THE NUMBERS

As of March 2020, more than 100,000 first responders and survivors were enrolled in government programs for treatment of 9/11-related illnesses.

site. Many people also struggled with mental health issues from the trauma they experienced on 9/11. The VCF covered their treatments. In 2015, Obama reauthorized the VCF again.

During his time in office, Obama commemorated eight 9/11 anniversaries. In 2009, he designated September 11 as a National Day of Service and Remembrance. The president called on all Americans to perform acts of service each year on that day. This was to honor the victims of the 9/11 terrorist attacks as well as first responders and US soldiers.

On the tenth anniversary of the 9/11 terrorist attacks, Obama visited memorials in Pennsylvania and at the Pentagon. He also attended a ceremony at Ground Zero. There, he was joined by former president Bush. The presidents stood side by side as the name of each 9/11 victim was read aloud.

President Trump

President Donald Trump took office on January 20, 2017. On the anniversary of the 9/11 terrorist attacks, he attended a ceremony at the Pentagon. On July 29, 2019, Trump signed a bill that made the VCF active through October 1, 2090. This would cover those affected by the 9/11 terrorist attacks for the rest of their lives.

When Trump took office, the United States was still involved in Iraq and Afghanistan. US troops had redeployed to Iraq in 2014 to fight the Islamic State of Iraq and Syria (ISIS). By 2020, thousands of troops remained in Iraq to control violence there. And in Afghanistan, the Taliban continued to attack US and Afghan forces.

From 2011 to 2013, the Obama administration had organized peace talks with the Taliban to end the war in Afghanistan. Unfortunately, the talks failed to produce an agreement. In 2018, the Trump administration reopened peace talks with the Taliban. They went on for months. At certain points, it looked like they might fail once again.

However, on February 29, 2020, the United States signed a peace agreement with the Taliban. The Taliban said it would stop supporting terrorist groups in Afghanistan. It also agreed to begin

Trump signed the VCF bill in the Rose Garden at the White House, surrounded by first responders and their families.

negotiations with the Afghan government. In return, the United States agreed to withdraw its last troops from Afghanistan.

In the summer of 2020, US troops began to leave Afghanistan. Some officials worried that without US troops, the Taliban would once again try to take over the country. However, many hoped that Afghanistan was on a path to peace.

The peace agreement was signed by US Special Representative Zalmay Khalilzad (*left*), and Mullah Abdul Ghani Baradar, a Taliban leader.

Leaders' Lasting Effects

After the 9/11 terrorist attacks, federal and local leaders did their best to respond to the crisis. They comforted survivors and honored victims. They rebuilt what had been destroyed. And, they tried to ensure that the United States would never face another terror threat.

The decisions that American leaders made in response to the 9/11 terrorist attacks changed the United States forever. There were new laws meant to protect Americans. And the United States engaged in two long wars. Some of these outcomes were, and continue to be, controversial. In January 2021, Joe Biden became the fourth president to serve since the 9/11 terrorist attacks. He continued the work begun by the leaders before him.

Many lives were instantly and painfully changed on September 11, 2001. Twenty years after the attacks, 9/11-related reforms, laws, and wars have permanently reshaped the United States. Today, there is a new generation of Americans who do not have direct memories of that fateful day and its aftermath. Many of these young Americans will one day become the nation's leaders. They will learn from the successes and failures of past leaders and work to ensure the continued security of the United States and the safety of all Americans.

Several million people visit the 9/11 Memorial Museum in New York City each year.

TIMELINE

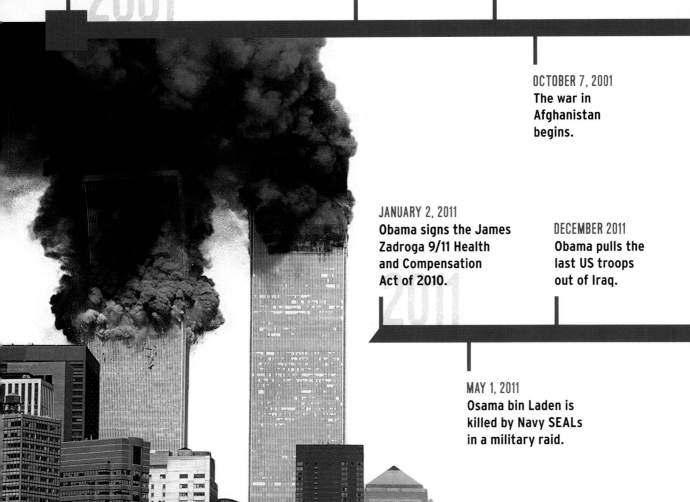

SEPTEMBER 11, 2001
Nearly 3,000 people die in the 9/11 terrorist attacks. President Bush addresses the nation, reassuring Americans that the country is still strong, and promising to find those responsible for the attacks.

SEPTEMBER 20, 2001
Bush announces the war on terror.

SEPTEMBER 22, 2001
Bush appoints Tom Ridge director of the new Office of Homeland Security.

2001

OCTOBER 7, 2001
The war in Afghanistan begins.

JANUARY 2, 2011
Obama signs the James Zadroga 9/11 Health and Compensation Act of 2010.

DECEMBER 2011
Obama pulls the last US troops out of Iraq.

2011

MAY 1, 2011
Osama bin Laden is killed by Navy SEALs in a military raid.

MARCH 2003
US troops invade Iraq.

2006
Saddam Hussein is executed after being found guilty of crimes against humanity.

NOVEMBER 2002
Bush forms the 9/11 Commission.

JULY 2004
The 9/11 Commission releases the *Final Report of the National Commission on Terrorist Attacks Upon the United States.*

2009
President Obama designates September 11 as a National Day of Service and Remembrance.

JULY 29, 2019
President Trump reauthorizes the September 11th Victim Compensation Fund through October 1, 2090.

JANUARY 2021
Joe Biden becomes the fourth US president to serve since the 9/11 terrorist attacks.

2014
US troops return to Iraq to fight ISIS.

FEBRUARY 29, 2020
The United States signs a peace agreement with the Taliban.

GLOSSARY

aftermath—the time immediately following a bad and usually destructive event.

analysis—an explanation of the nature and meaning of something.

bipartisan—involving cooperation, agreement, and compromise between two political parties.

cabinet—a group of advisors chosen by the president to lead government departments.

civilian—of or relating to something nonmilitary. A civilian is a person who is not an active member of the military.

commemorate—to honor and remember an important person or event.

deploy—to spread out and organize in a battle formation.

dictator—a ruler with complete control who often governs in a cruel way.

domestic—of, relating to, or made in one's own country.

hijack—to take over by threatening violence.

infrastructure—the basic framework of public society. It includes a community's government, transportation, and education systems.

Iraq War—a conflict that began in March 2003 when the United States and its allies invaded Iraq. After the fall of the Iraqi government, US troops remained in Iraq to help stabilize the new government.

Islam—the religion of Muslims as described in the Koran. Islam is based on the teachings of the god Allah through the prophet Muhammad.

landmark—an important structure of historical or physical interest.

legacy—something important or meaningful handed down from previous generations or from the past.

memorial—something that serves to remind people of a person or an event.

monitor—to watch, keep track of, or oversee.

Muslim—a person who follows Islam.

negotiation—a discussion to work out an agreement about the terms of something.

nonpartisan—not supporting one political party or group over another.

Pentagon—the five-sided building near Washington, DC, where the main offices of the US Department of Defense are located.

stronghold—an area dominated by a particular group.

trauma—a wound or injury to the body or the mind.

ONLINE RESOURCES

Booklinks
NONFICTION NETWORK
FREE! ONLINE NONFICTION RESOURCES

To learn more about American leadership after 9/11, please visit **abdobooklinks.com** or scan this QR code. These links are routinely monitored and updated to provide the most current information available.

INDEX